The "Other" Is My Neighbour

The "Other" Is My Neighbour

*Developing an Ecumenical Response
to Migration*

**World Council
of Churches**
Publications

THE "OTHER" IS MY NEIGHBOUR
Developing an Ecumenical Response to Migration

WCC Publications is the book publishing programme of the World Council of Churches. Founded in 1948, the WCC promotes Christian unity in faith, witness and service for a just and peaceful world. A global fellowship, the WCC brings together more than 345 Protestant, Orthodox, Anglican and other churches representing more than 550 million Christians in 110 countries and works cooperatively with the Roman Catholic Church.

Opinions expressed in WCC Publications are those of the authors.

Cover design: Ann-Katrin Hergert
Cover image: Multicultural Faces © Geoff Allan. Used by permission.
ISBN: 978-2-8254-1605-1

World Council of Churches
150 route de Ferney, P.O. Box 2100
1211 Geneva 2, Switzerland
http://publications.oikoumene.org

CONTENTS

ACKNOWLEDGMENTS

This document is the result of an extensive process of consultation, research and dialogue over a period of sixteen months, with regional ecumenical organizations, member churches, related ecumenical organizations, activists and theologians. A working group of theologians drawn from different regions and experiences served as a working group, and out of this group a drafting committee was formed to compose this work. The document would not have been possible without the commitment and tireless work by the theologians' working group. Therefore a special thanks and deep appreciation go to the members of the theological working group:

Rev. Dr Drea Fröchtling, Apst. Adejare Oyewole, Dr Gert Noort, Rev. Dr Luis Rivera-Pagàn, Ms Sara S. Kaulule, Rev. Asora Amosa, Rev. Goyo De la Cruz, Rev. Robert Hamd, Mr Joseph Robert Ledger Moloney, Ms Doris Peschke, Ms Vivi Akakpo, Ms Seta Hedashian, Ms Aguinaco Carmen, Ms Alvarez Coleman Ofelia, Rev. Dr Daniel Chetti, Dr Maarardzo Elizabeth Mutambara, Dr Victoria Kamondji, Fr. Maurizio Pettenà, Dr Susanna Snyder, Mr Mervin Toquero, Bishop Stephen N. Mwangi, Mr Micheal Blair, Rev. Milton Mejia, Rev. Nora Colmenares, Rev. Dr Roswitha Golder, Ms Sharon Rose Joy Ruiz Duremdes, Rev. Corazon C. Abugan, Rev. Fr. Rex R. B. Reyes and Ms Maria Koutazi.

Special mention and recognition go to the drafting team, who worked tirelessly to produce the first, second, third, fourth drafts and the final document that went for editing. To the three members of the drafting team: *Dr Drea Fröchtling, Mr Joseph Robert Ledger Moloney and Dr Gert Noort,* we say thank you for your patience, your passion for the issues discussed, your care and your commitment. Accept our prayers as a form of sincere gratitude.

Ms Miriam Reidy Prost for her careful and detailed work in editing and finalising the text for publication.

Rev. Dr Deenabandhu Manchala and Ms Sydia Nduna for their ontribution, insights, support and for facilitating the process that led to the publication.

INTRODUCTION

Throughout 2011 and 2012, representatives from churches and church-related organizations as well as several migration networks met to consider the theme "Who is my neighbour? Migration and the ecclesial landscape – an ecumenical response to migration." For this purpose, three consultations were held: in Beirut, Lebanon (5-7 December 2011), Geneva, Switzerland (7-9 May 2012) and Manila, the Philippines (4-11 November 2012).

The consultations were organized by the World Council of Churches (WCC) as a regional and global meeting of the Global Ecumenical Network on Migration (GEM). The GEM meeting is always carried out in partnership with one of the members of the network comprising the All Africa Conference of Churches (AACC), the Churches' Commission for Migrants in Europe (CCME) and the Middle East Council of Churches (MECC), Pacific Conference of Churches (PCC), Christian Conference of Asia (CCA), Latin American Council of Churches (CLAI), National Council of Churches in Australia (NACC) and the Ecumenical Initiative for Justice (KAIROS). These consultations aim at "assist[ing] the churches and the ecumenical organizations in their calling to be the church amidst the phenomenon of increasing diversity of people, language, cultures, ethnicity and religions."[1]

At each consultation, responses to migration issues from regional contexts from all over the world were explored. Each was followed by a second smaller gathering of the Theological Working Group, which dealt specifically with the theological and ecclesiological consequences of the findings of the various regions. Issues that provided structure and focus for our theological debate included:

> the ways in which we view or understand ourselves and "others"; the moral imperative of holding powers accountable for the present economic policies that thrive on the abuse of human beings and the creation; and practical

---

[1] *"Who is my neighbour?" Migration and the ecclesial landscape: An ecumenical response to migration*, WCC concept paper, 2012, 1.

steps to encourage and equip congregations to become just and inclusive communities.[2]

This document is the result of the deliberations at all the meetings. It is written from the joint perspective of migrant churches and established historic congregations. This document is divided into three sections. The first section explores the biblical and theological insights related to migration. The second section identifies the subsequent ecclesiological implications of migration on the ecclesial landscape and for the nature and mission of the church itself. The third section calls for a renewed ecumenical response to migration in the light of the WCC 2013 Assembly theme, "God of life, lead us to justice and peace." The volume concludes with an appendix that offers an assessment of the migration phenomenon and discusses its several facets and ambiguities.

As Christians, We Hold These Convictions

1. We affirm the sacredness of all human life and the sanctity of creation

"In the beginning when God created the heavens and the earth … And God saw that it was good … So God created humankind in his image …"

All people are made in the image of God. Respect for the human dignity and the worth of every person regardless of age, abilities, ethnicity, gender, class, nationality, race and religion is foundational to our faith. Our faith compels us to ensure that human life, physical security and personal safety are upheld in law and institutions.

---

[2] Ibid.

2. The biblical values of love, justice and peace compel us to renew Christian response to the marginalized and excluded.

"'You shall love the Lord your God with all your heart, and with all your soul, and with all your mind.' This is the greatest and first commandment. And the second is like it: 'You shall love your neighbour as yourself.'" (Matthew 22:37-39)

The realm of God is a vision of a just and united world. The challenge of prophesy and of Jesus' teaching is to liberate and equip Christians to have the courage to work for alternative community, to work for peace and justice, which is to address the causes which uproot people... There is no peace without justice or full justice without peace. (Amos 5:24) Our faith compels us to struggle for justice and peace for all; to work for a world where economic, political and social institutions serve people rather than the other way around.

3. The biblical challenge to build inclusive community requires us to accompany the uprooted in service and witness.

"So then you are no longer strangers and aliens, but you are citizens with the saints and also members of the household of God." (Ephesians 2:19)

Christians are called to be with the oppressed, the marginalized and the excluded in their suffering, their struggles and their hopes. A ministry of accompaniment and advocacy with uprooted people upholds the principles of prophetic witness and service – *diaconia*. We cannot desert the "needy," nor set boundaries to compassion. (Hebrews 13:2, Luke 10:25-37, Jeremiah 5-7)

Rationale

The Central Committee of the World Council of Churches on September 22, 1995 unanimously adopted a statement on uprooted people, "A Moment to Choose: Risking to Be with Uprooted People." The issues they grappled with are as relevant today as they were at that time. Some excerpts from this statement are reproduced on the facing page.

Challenges and Opportunities

Migration poses a number of challenges and opportunities for Christian communities looking to God to lead them toward justice and peace today. How will migration change the relationship we have with our neighbours, and indeed, whom do we see as our neighbours? How can churches overcome the tendency of "othering" the outsiders? What is the nature of the global and local communities that we as Christians want to bring into being? What are the principles that will guide us to justice, peace and the integrity of creation as we face the challenges of migration? How can the "other" be fully included? How might we understand and re-imagine the very nature and mission of the church in the light of the migration context we have outlined? What does the Christian tradition offer in terms of ethical guidelines and experiences with migration?

Sold for 300 Dollars

It has been quite a journey from being just an Overseas Filipino Worker [OFW] in Korea to what I am now: a firm advocate/activist for migrants' rights. It was in June, 1991 when I embarked on a new chapter of my life as an OFW in Korea.

I am the ninth of 13 children, thus it was difficult for my parents to send us all to school. I couldn't get a job that would pay decent wages so I planned to go abroad. I found a recruiter who found me a job in South Korea. When my passport was handed to me, the information regarding my age, address and date of birth had been changed. Since I had paid the recruiter a huge amount of money (Php 45,000 or $2,400) which I had borrowed, I kept silent. I was 20 years old at that time.

We were ordered to proceed to Window 5 at the immigration line, where we were waved through without any questions straight to boarding the plane. It was the same thing when we arrived in South Korea: to go through a specific immigration booth, where we were just waved through and immediately whisked to our hotel. There was a selection process going on and for every man selected, an envelope of money was given to the recruiter as payment.

On the very first day of work, we were forced to work for 12-14 hours without any rest or sufficient food. I received a salary much smaller than what was promised. I had no overtime pay and we worked seven days a week with 14-hour shifts. I realized that I was an undocumented worker, and as such, could not complain as we were not legal. Because of this, I confronted my employer only to find out that he bought me from my recruiter for $300.

At the embassy, I discovered that there were so many of us Filipino workers who were undocumented and were being exploited and maltreated. Some were even physically abused. The response of the embassy officials angered and horrified me: these officials called us "stupid" and a "shame" to our country.

I was able to become a migrants' rights advocate when I became involved in my church. I started feeling like a human again and not a machine. It was also my work with the church where I saw the magnitude of the problem of migrants, particularly undocumented migrant workers, I saw how they were being hunted like animals, and some died while trying to escape immigration authorities.

After 12 years in South Korea, I was found out by immigration police and was deported.

1. BIBLICAL AND THEOLOGICAL INSIGHTS

1. As Christian churches grapple with the steep questions posed by the contemporary migration context, they can turn first to the strong biblical themes concerning migration, the "other" and the church.

"Strangers" on the Move

2. The biblical writings, partly going back to times of exile and migration, are ambivalent about the migratory experience. The biblical stories and ethical guidelines reflect that leaving one's country can be a road either to freedom (Exodus 14:19ff) or to slavery (Genesis 37:28). The Scriptures speak of both hardships and new chances, of injustice as well as restored life. They show the migration experience in its complexity and ambiguity: it can be a blessing or a curse, a right to enjoy or an injustice too harsh to endure. Therefore, the biblical witness does not categorically denounce or affirm migration. Rather, it provides narratives that inform our conversation on the biblical texts, indicating that all peoples created in the image of God deserve to be treated with dignity and as recipients of justice.

3. The book of Genesis highlights a range of archetypal human migratory experiences. Cain became a displaced person, and people migrated to the cities as the centres of power. Noah and his family were forced to leave the place of their origin due to a natural disaster. Abraham and Sarah, ancestors of the faith, are described as people who are "called out." They left their home for a new unknown place that God claimed he would show them in time (Genesis 12:1), while Abraham and Lot realized that the land they lived on was insufficient to meet the needs of different extended families (Genesis 13:1-18). Neighbouring countries became a destination for survival in periods of crop failure and famine (e.g., Genesis 12:10; 26:1; 41:57).

4. Foundational stories of faith, such as the story about the Israelites who escaped slavery in Egypt, worshipped God in a portable sanctuary (Exodus 26) and travelled to the Promised Land, refer to experiences of migration (Exodus 12ff.). While the experience of

leaving Egypt and nomadic life in the desert marked the identity of the people of God, the Scriptures also recognize that people on the move need something more permanent. The people of Israel fostered hope to have land and to enjoy the fruits of their labour (Leviticus 25:38, Isaiah 65:22).

5. The Mosaic laws for life in the Promised Land were intended to create a safe place for all (Leviticus 25:18). The laws provided protection for widows and orphans, for those who lost their land and were therefore forced to migrate. Leviticus 25 introduces the Year of Jubilee, in which all properties should be returned to the original owners. Proprietors are admonished to keep in mind that God is the sole proprietor of land and that people are aliens and guests in God's country (Leviticus 25:23). The circle of poverty and forced migration and internal displacement was thereby to be broken, so that life could be affirmed.

Violent Expelling from the Land: Colombia

In Colombia, communities formed by indigenous, African descent and *campesino* (farmer) groups in the Uraba region were violently expelled from their ancestral territory by a transnational economic project for the production of agro-fuel.

Today, these communities are returning to their territory thanks to the intervention of Christian and human rights organizations that accompanied them in order to rebuild their lives and their indigenous culture. In this way, they are also recovering the biodiversity of their territories that was being destroyed by large palm oil plantations.

---

6. Turning to the New Testament, movement, travel and exile are shown to be central aspects of the life of Jesus. Jesus is often referred to as an outsider – for example, the one for whom there is no room in the inn (Luke 2:7), the refugee and immigrant in Egypt (Matthew 2:13), the man who has "nowhere to lay his head" (Luke 9:58). As the word incarnate, God in human flesh, Jesus can be described as a

divine migrant who crossed borders between heaven and earth. During his life, while travelling from town to town, he challenged the validity of ethnic and cultural barriers, as is visible in his encounters with Samaritans. Movement from one place to the other also characterized the life of Jesus' disciples. They were called to leave their homes (e.g., Matthew 4:19) and according to tradition, they travelled to distant lands to proclaim the gospel. In light of the Book of Acts, it is not perhaps surprising that the early Christians are referred to as those on/of the way (Acts 9:2) and that movement and concepts of exile also featured prominently in the emerging church. Christians are described by the author of 1 Peter as "aliens and exiles" (1 Peter 2:11). Alienation and migration thus are identity marks of God's chosen people (1 Peter 2:9).

7. Theologically speaking, migration as being dispersed (*diaspora*) and alienated is therefore a mark of the church (*nota ecclesiae*). This culminates in the Letter to the Hebrews, which underlines that believers are pilgrims who "have no lasting city but are looking for the city that is to come" (Hebrews 13:14). From this perspective, all human beings, residents with or without a migration background, are "foreigners." Our identities are constructed in an in-between: in-between paradise lost and the heavenly Jerusalem, in-between cross, resurrection and the second coming of Christ, in-between ethnic or gender identity and the larger body of Christ, in-between despair and hope. In the local Christian communities, pilgrims find temporary residence, a home for the homeless, where they experience comfort, share hope and struggle together while trusting in the promise of a new creation. Thus, a primary metaphor the Bible uses throughout describes the relationship of the people of God to the world they live in as resident aliens. This means that Christians throughout the centuries have lived in tension with the socio-political context, causing them not to remain inward-focused, but rather outwardly-seeking to faithfully live out the gospel.

The "Other" as the Image of God

8. That the Scriptures refer to followers of Jesus as "aliens and exiles" implies that migration in itself is not viewed as an experience to be aspired to. Much rather, it calls us to justly and inclusively relate to others who equally experience alienation. It thus provides an ethical mandate for the way we perceive and respond to the presence of the other. It invites us to faithfully align ourselves with the eschatological perspective of journeying with the nations ("others") to the Messianic banquet in the heavenly Jerusalem (Isaiah 25:6). It is *with* the nations that we sojourn and will sit at the banquet table. It is also *with* the other that we hope for justice and deliverance from forces of death (Isaiah 25:8; 26:9). The other is included in the eschatological perspective and in the cry that God will raise the hand against the power of violent and unjust oppressors.

9. While disconcerting expressions of exclusion and racism can be found in biblical narratives, especially in the stories of the land conquest and the exilic period, many passages call upon the Israelite people to care for and support the "alien." The alien should not just be tolerated but loved (Leviticus 19:34). Food and clothing should be provided, wages of the poor and needy should not be withheld (Deuteronomy 24:14). Religious leaders were summoned to uphold justice, especially in relation to those who were vulnerable – widows, foreigners, orphans (Jeremiah 7:6, cf. Exodus 23:9 and Deuteronomy 24:18). Psalm 146:9, written during the exilic period, exemplifies that God watches over the foreigners. The reference to a God who supports migrants in their plight and who sees to an end of their exploitation became the very core of the covenant relation (Exodus 3:7-8; 22:21).

10. The ethical mandate "love your neighbour as yourself" (Leviticus 19:18, Matthew 19:19) reflects that all were created in God's image. Being the image of God is a relational issue, particularly so in the light of the Trinity. Human beings and the world are God's (Genesis 1:26). We are related to God, but also to others. All of us mirror God's being. In the context of migration, this notion of *imago Dei* affirms the unbreakable interrelatedness of God, human beings and the world. Theologically, it is generally used to emphasize the

essential equality, value and unbreakable relationship between human beings, other human beings and God. On the other hand, it points to the richness, the unity and the diversity of God's creation and, consequently, the respect required for it. The notion of being in the image of God thus empowers us to relate respectfully and in an embracing manner to all sojourners, to all people who migrate. Christianity's claim that all were equal before God and all equally precious to him impacted the formation of the early church and Greco-Roman society. Christian communities became a harbour to women, who had always been kept in the shadows, and to slaves, who had never before been recognized as having social dignity or political importance.

11. The "Golden Rule" – "Do to others as you would have them do to you" (Luke 6:31) – implies that we need to uphold each and every person's dignity. Furthermore, the divine command "Love your neighbour as yourself" reminds us of the fact that the inclusive kingdom of God knows no human-made barriers, no foreigners and no "others." It provides a place for people who are "neighbours" to one another, equally part of the kingdom-community, equally gifted with talents.

The "Other" and the Community

12. As Christians, we affirm that the church, the communion of believers, is one through the redemptive work of Christ (Galatians 3:28). Therefore, those who are baptized are joined together as brothers and sisters. We acknowledge that no part of the body can be rejected and no part can claim to be the most important. As the apostle Paul wrote to the multi-ethnic congregation in the city of Corinth: "For in the one Spirit we were all baptized into one body – Jews or Greeks, slaves or free – and we were all made to drink of one Spirit." (1 Corinthians 12:13). The one constant and unchangeable reality for the church is the oneness of the body of Christ of whom all followers of Christ are members.

13. While we affirm this unity of the church, we also recognize its great diversity. Though the church is grounded in the one word of God, it has become manifest in diverse ways.[1] It is indeed fair to say that cultural and theological diversity has been a characteristic of Christ's church from its very inception. Thus, "There is no longer Jew or Greek, there is no longer slave or free, there is no longer male and female; for all of you are one in Christ Jesus" (Galatians 3:28) does not mean that the church rejects or denies distinct religious or ethnic identities as members of the wider society. Rather, it embodies them within the vision of a new creation in which diversity is celebrated and unity experienced, while mutuality and interdependence of life are affirmed. In other words, the church is the promise of a new eschatological community, sojourning with the nations to the heavenly Jerusalem for the Messianic banquet (Isaiah 2:2; 25:6). It lives by Paul's word, "For he is our peace; in his flesh he has made both groups into one and has broken down the dividing wall, that is, the hostility between us" (Ephesians 2: 14).

14. Cultural differences may be experienced as a threat to one's own values. Indeed, the presence of the "other" questions our way of living and our worldview. Yet we may remember that the "other" also defines us. It is in relation to the other that we clarify our identity and value as well as evaluate our convictions. Christians, as pilgrims on the way to the Messianic banquet, view identity and otherness in the light of the kingdom that is to come. Our identity is determined by our communion with Christ and being part of the kingdom-community. This identity embraces diversity as much as it celebrates unity.[2]

15. Unity and diversity are not only visible in the church, but they can also be found in God, in God's trinitarian way of being and interacting. The Father is different from the Son, as much as the Son is different from the Father and the Spirit, and yet they are united in a life-enhancing difference and in loving relationship. As a pilgrim community, we "believe in the Triune God who is the creator,

---

[1] *The Nature and Mission of the Church: A Stage on the Way to a Common Statement*, Faith and Order Paper 198, WCC, Geneva, 2005, 4.

[2] "The dialogue between faith and culture," talk given by John Paul II at Sogang University, Seoul, South Korea, May 5, 1985. *Text in Origins* Vol. 14, No. 2, 21.

redeemer and sustainer of life. God created the whole *oikoumene* in his image and constantly works in the world to affirm and safeguard life. We believe in Jesus Christ, the life of the world, the incarnation of God's love for the world (John 3:16). Affirming life in all its fullness is Jesus Christ's ultimate concern and mission (John 10:10). We believe in God, the Holy Spirit, the life-giver, who sustains and empowers life and renews the whole creation (Genesis 2:7; John 3:8)."[3]

The "Other" and God-Given Resources

16. While we hold that God empowers life and renews creation, we acknowledge that the earth pays the price of the sinfulness of people (Romans 8:22, Isaiah 24:4-13). Instead of the renewal of creation, the earth that was entrusted to us is often misused and human beings are exploited. We need to recognize that the God-given resources of the earth are to be used for the benefit of all. God's gift is not exclusively meant for a privileged minority; the earth is God's creation and treasured "possession." All that exists was created by God and it was good (Genesis 1:31, Psalm 24:1). God blessed human beings to enjoy the earth and to care for her (Genesis 1:28). This calls us to acknowledge that we live in interdependence with creation. Stewardship of the earth and concrete steps toward eco-justice are nothing less than the recognition that creation is God's and the resources are for all to be enjoyed.

The "Other" as a Member

17. The "other" is not just tolerated in the kingdom of God, but has an active role to play and a unique contribution to make. In the prophetic writings, we find that the nations are drawn to Zion by God's light and bring their wealth as a tribute to God's reign (Isaiah 60: 5-11). Foreigners will rebuild the city walls; their kings will serve the new kingdom (Isaiah 60:10). In the description of the future of Zion, the tribute by the nations is mentioned in parallel with peace

---

[3] *Together towards life: Mission and Evangelism in changing landscapes*, WCC Commission on World Mission and Evangelism, 2012, par. 1.

that flows to the city (Isaiah 66:10). All nations and all tongues will come to see God's glory (Isaiah 66:18), not just the children of Abraham.

18. The gospels remind us as well that the "other" contributes. In Luke's account of the people who were cured of leprosy, it was the excluded Samaritan who came back to bring tribute to Jesus and who was saved by his faith (Luke 17:16-19). The Syro-Phoenician woman challenged Jesus to reckon with the Gentiles and include them in his ministry (John 4). The Roman soldier, a foreigner who understood that Jesus did not have to travel in order to heal his slave, contributed greatly by becoming an exemplary believer who was almost "obviously" included in the Kingdom of Heaven and the eschatological meal (Matthew 8:8-11). Recognizing the contributions of the "other" to the life of the community creates space for inclusion and mutuality.

The United Church of Christ in the Philippines: A Pilgrim Community

The United Church of Christ in the Philippines (UCCP) is a pilgrim community. The UCCP in its statement of faith declares that: We believe… In the church, the one body of Christ the community of those reconciled to God through Jesus Christ and entrusted with Jesus' own ministry.

We believe… Man is created in the image of God, sinful and destined to live in the community with God, entrusted with God's creation and called to participate in the establishment of a meaningful and just social order. Our statement of faith has guided us in our giving worth, honour and respect to persons and people as they are created in the image of God, whoever they are and wherever they come from.

It is on this premise that the UCCP opens its door through the programme of caring and ministering to the Indonesian individuals and families who have come to our land. They were Christian Indonesian farmers and fishermen whohave come to our shore in the Balot and Sarangani islands. They were landless in their own country, searching for greener pastures. In the late 70's, they were just few, but as the years went on, they increased in numbers and local churches have been organized in their committees so that in 1986, they were recognized as legitimate participants and members of the UCCP and integrated with the South Cotabato-Sarangani District Conference.

These Indonesian churches continue to grow. Last April during the Annual Conference in session of South Cotabato-Sarangani District Conference, 23 Indonesian local churches participated. With our faith journey as a church, we work together irrespective of colour, age, gender, profession and nationality. We appreciate everyone's contribution in their participation in building the Kingdom of God where love, justice and peace prevail.

2. ECCLESIOLOGICAL IMPLICATIONS

Migration and the Ecclesial Landscape

19. Migration is greatly impacting all major religions throughout the world. Of the total number of global migrants, an estimated 106 million (49 percent) are Christian and almost 60 million (27 percent) are Muslims. The remaining quarter is a mix of Hindus (5 percent), Buddhists (3 percent), Jews (2 percent), other faiths (4 percent) or the religiously unaffiliated (9 percent).[1] Christian migrants' main region of origin is Europe (44 percent) followed by Latin and Central America (30 percent) and Asia-Pacific (13 percent). The largest single movement involves over 12 million Christians from Mexico, mostly migrating to the United States. The major destination regions for Christian emigrants are Europe (38 percent), North America (34 percent) and Asia-Pacific (11 percent).[2] These large movements of people across the globe alter the ecclesial landscapes in a number of ways – such as increasing local denominational numbers and ethnic diversity in membership, the formation of "migrant-churches" and introducing challenges related to theological hermeneutics and ecclesiology.

20. Migration leads to increasing cultural, theological and linguistic pluralism within Christian practice. While many Middle East Christians recently emigrated to other parts of the world, some 2,350,000 Christians mostly from India, the Philippines, North America and Europe immigrated into the region. These Christians settled as migrant workers in the six Gulf Cooperation Council countries (Bahrain, Kuwait, Oman, Qatar, Saudi Arabia, the United Arab Emirates), and worship in multicultural congregations.[3] Inhabitants of the Sarangani Islands in the Philippines have witnessed the growth of 23 local Indonesian churches, following the immigration of Indonesian farmers since the seventies. Geneva

---

[1] *Faith on the Move*, Pew Research Centre, 8 March 2012.
[2] *Faith on the Move*, Pew Research Centre, 8 March 2012.
[3] *Faith on the Move*, Pew Research Centre, 8 March 2012.

(Switzerland) had over 90 worshipping communities of foreign origin, usually small Pentecostal churches, African Independent churches, Charismatic and Evangelical communities by the end of 2007. By the end of 2008, Ireland had 361 migrant-led churches and chaplaincies. The largest group, the Redeemed Christian Church of God, operated 70 different centres for worship. The platform of migrant churches in Rotterdam (the Netherlands) recorded over 110 migrant churches in 2007. The majority of these worshipped in a language other than Dutch and ranged in membership from 40 groups with less than 50 members to five groups with over 500 members.[4] In 2006, a slowing rate of decline in church attendance in the United Kingdom was largely attributed to the influx of Christians from Africa and Europe, while in Norwich's Catholic Cathedral, hundreds of people from the Philippines, India and Africa have boosted the average weekend attendance from 800 up to 1200.[5]

21. Migrant newcomers can play a significant role to challenge a mono-cultural denomination long established in a particular nation-state to interact with and sometimes adopt different ways of being church, expressing faith, worshipping, praying and relating to one another. For example, in many parts of the world, members of "national churches" and mainline denominations now worship alongside migrant Christians who have established multicultural or ethnic-majority congregations. In these newly emerging churches, many languages are used, often different from the languages used by established ("national") churches. A German Lutheran could find herself alongside a Korean Lutheran, or a Latin American Catholic alongside an Irish Catholic. The situation of these churches is fluid as is the process of migration itself: churches may grow through new mission activity, or merge as well as separate. These changes are an indication of the mission of God working itself out as Christians seek to be faithful witnesses to the gospel. Indeed, increasing oscillation between "national" identities and internationalism is challenged, and re-denominationalism and post-denominational Christian globalism

---

[4] R. Calvert, *Gids voor Christelijke Migranten Gemeenschappen in Rotterdam*, Rotterdam, 2007.
[5] Archbishop Silvano M. Tomasi, Apostolic Nuncio, Permanent Observer of the Holy See to the United Nations and Other International Organizations in Geneva, appears in *Thinking Migration* No. 1, 2011, 16.

occur. Nevertheless, the fact remains that human beings desire community to express religious beliefs through worship, fellowship and shared communion. This indicates that migrant newcomers create capacity for new and shared expressions of their Christian faith.

Nature and Mission of the Church

22. The Faith and Order Paper *The Nature and Mission of the Church* (2005) affirms that:

> It is God's design, to gather all creation under the Lordship of Christ (cf. Ephesians 1:10) and to bring humanity and all creation into all communion [...] As persons who acknowledge Jesus Christ as Lord and savior, Christians are called to proclaim the gospel in word and deed [...] They are called to live the values of the reign of God and to be a foretaste of the reign in the world. Mission thus belongs to the very being of the church [...] In exercising its mission, the church cannot be true to itself without giving witness (*martyria*) to God's will for the salvation and transformation of the world.[6]

23. Thus, mission constitutes a "response in love to the call of the Triune God for a journey in faith and hope for a new world of justice, peace and life for all."[7] It is about "the church embodying God's salvation in this world."[8] Mission is transformative, inclusive and justice-oriented and is grounded in the Trinity. The prime actors in mission are not human beings, the church or a missionary organization, but the Triune God. God in God's own self is a life of communion, and God's mission draws humanity and creation into communion with God's life (cf. John 21).[9] God's mission is aimed at communion, at a life of fullness, justice and peace in conjunction with the source of all creation.

---

[6] *The Nature and Mission of the Church*, WCC, Geneva, 9-10.
[7] *Together towards life: Mission and Evangelism in changing landscapes*, CWME, Geneva 2012, par. 107.
[8] *Together towards life*, par. 103.
[9] *Together towards life*, par. 19.

24. Migration profoundly impacts both the *nature* and the *mission* of the church, given that nature and mission are inextricably bound together. We believe that the role of the church is to strive to be a place for all and a welcoming community for all peoples and nations. This has been the nature of the *ecclesia* since its very inception. This is part and parcel of the *missio Dei*.

25. The following paragraphs will take up essential notions from the previous section such as "pilgrim community," "kingdom community" and "inclusive community." They will define the nature as well as the mission of the church in the light of migration and will highlight the implications for a *missio Dei* that takes its lead from a saviour who was once considered a refugee in Egypt.

The Church as a Pilgrim Community: Called to Transgress Boundaries

26. The early church, living in a multireligious and multicultural context, clearly defined itself as a "pilgrim church" by nature. Clement, bishop of Rome used this definition in his famous letter to the congregation in Corinth.[10] It is the journey of faith that all pilgrims have in common. Pilgrims are *en route,* are sojourners and pilgrims (1 Peter 2:11). Those who seek to follow Christ are on the move, as the incarnated Christ himself had no place to lay his head (Matthew 8:20). They have their citizenship in heaven (Philippians 3:20), knowing that their true treasure is not to be found on earth (Luke 18:22). Being *en route* as a pilgrim, realizing the resident yet alien status of Christians and Christian communities, lies at the heart of Christian faith from the very inception of the church. Becoming a pilgrim therefore is the calling of each individual Christian. Becoming a pilgrim community is the calling of the church.

27. In our times, this notion that the one church is by nature a pilgrim community needs to be rediscovered in order to gain new self-understanding of Christian (communal) identity. The ecclesial landscape, especially in migrant-receiving countries, has changed rapidly. The co-existence of migration-shaped congregations and

---

[10] K.M. George, *The Early Church: Defending the faith, witness and proclamation: patristic perspectives.* Geneva 1996, 23-24.

local churches challenges the church to rethink its nature in the light of migration and pilgrimage. The church is one, yet diverse; it is local yet in pilgrimage; it provides comfort for those who seek shelter yet it moves people to act prophetically. A church that is in pilgrimage is not static, but dynamic and "becoming" in nature.

28. The notion of being a pilgrim community in nature has implications for the contextual mission of the church as well. The boundaries of the church need to be reframed with regard to nationhood, language, ethnicity, status and leadership. A church in pilgrimage is, for example, aware of fellow travellers who have an equal right to finding shelter, justice, job opportunities, participation rights, access to places of worship, education, residence and contextual identity. It points toward "an active partnership with God in speaking truth to powers, confronting and transforming unjust, inhuman, discriminatory ideologies, cultures and realities, so that the world may be what God always wanted it to be."[11] Although the apostle Paul insisted on his rights as a Roman citizen, he nevertheless worked out his missiology (2 Cor 6: 3-10) as a citizen of the world, recognizing a borderless kingdom of God. His concern was for the welfare of all people. As churches, we are called to overcome those elemental forces that are life-destroying and harm migrants by identifying them as the other. We remind ourselves that our mission is spiritual, grounded in Christ who transcends all boundaries.

29. While we affirm that the mission is God's, we understand that it is God who calls us, pilgrims in this world, to participate in mission. We do so by announcing the coming of the kingdom, by inviting all peoples, regardless of who they are, to come and follow Christ and by seeking *koinonia* (fellowship) with others. Authentic mission looks for "partners in pilgrimage," not "objects" of mission.

---

[11] *Global Platform for Theological Reflection 2010: Unity and Mission Today: Voices and Visions from the Margins.* Bucharest, Romania, October 4-10, 2010, 13.

The Church as a Kingdom Community:
Called to Challenge Injustice

30. The kingdom of God is a space beyond any human-made
geographical boundaries where justice and peace flow like a never-
ending stream, where kinship of the whole *oikoumene* is lived and
where the cross of the incarnate Christ encourages a life in mutual
relationships on a vertical as well as on a horizontal level. Kingdom
communities are communities in which there are "no longer strangers
and aliens, but ... members of the household of God" (Ephesians
2:19).

31. In the New Testament, Jesus shared the table and its gifts with the
marginalized. God's kingdom provides a space that is larger than any
national, ethnic or gender confines. It is a spiritual space, symbolized
in the image of the New Jerusalem with its emphasis on God's
dwelling among the people. It is a relational space as well, a kin-dom,
in which all people are related to each other. As a kingdom

community, the church aims at the humanization of society by transforming the cosmos in all its dimensions, structures and manifestations. Our common concern is to affirm life, overcome those elemental forces that are life-destroying, and to strive together toward the development of human dignity and well-being in the name of Christ.

32. The church is called to imagine and develop a migration-shaped mission, which is the essential being of the church. As migration is intrinsically linked to issues of injustice, missional work of the churches needs to involve itself in the struggle against social injustice. Our missiology needs to express itself as a deep commitment to the truth of the biblical message, practiced as good news to all peoples, through our active obedience to confront injustices within our contexts. The pilgrim church is, both in nature and mission, revolutionary and reconciliatory. It calls for conversion and repentance; it invites to discipleship and calls to worship. It goes beyond the programmes of aid and relief and challenges structures of societies that perpetuate injustice, oppression and alienation. In the midst of human suffering and unjust socio-political orders, the church is called to exercise the revolution of Christ: to replace the power of the world with the vulnerable power of the cross.

33.   Migration-shaped mission needs to take its ecclesiological starting point "from below." If it fails to do so, the nature of the church – being a pilgrim church and an inclusive community – is not taken seriously. Migration-shaped mission therefore seeks to embrace people at the margins as fellow travellers. In that perspective, it is not the inherited identities of nationalism, language and tradition, but the inclusive vision of God's reign that brings the church into being. It is the commitment to the values of justice, reconciliation, peace and compassion, dignity and life for all that gives the church its distinct identity as a called community. It was essentially this commitment that brought the Jesus community into being.

The Church as an Inclusive Community: Called to Be "Neighbours" to the Other

34. As Christians hold that the church is one in nature, it has been at the heart of the World Council of Churches "to proclaim the oneness of the church of Jesus Christ and to call the churches to the goal of visible unity in one faith and one eucharistic fellowship, expressed in worship and in common life in Christ, in order that the world may believe."[12]

35. This oneness of the body of Christ does not imply absence of difference in the church, but much rather maintaining and celebrating it. Diversity characterized the inception of the church, with inclusive practices being devised at an early stage. For example, throughout the Book of Acts, the multicultural and multilingual nature of God's people is clearly shown (Acts 6; 10:35-36; 15:16-17). Diversity was understood as a fact of life, and was theologically embraced as an enriching gift. As sojourners who follow Christ, we respect that we are called from many nations and constitute a diverse multi-ethnic communion, a safe space for encounter of fellow travellers, for mutual enrichment and critique where gifts to the ministry can flourish. The church forever shapes local contextual faith communities with members from all nations and all peoples and in that diversity, it offers worship, fellowship (*koinonia*) and witness (mission and *diakonia*). In doing so, it responds eschatologically to issues of injustice, exclusion and ethnic divisions.

36. The Christian pilgrim community of Christ values the crossing of boundaries, openness to cultural encounters, courage to face inevitable complexities and appreciation of differences as sources of strength. This makes hospitality, solidarity and humility central characteristics of being church and undertaking ministry.

37. The local congregation, where pilgrims are gathered around word and sacrament, is the place and space where people from diverse cultural and ethnic backgrounds meet in the name of Christ and where burdens and challenges are shared. Migration-shaped mission and

---

[12] *The Nature and Mission of the Church*, 1.

ministry, to all who are in need of Gods promises of life in fullness, can be developed in these ecclesial spaces.

38. In this context, a new ecclesial space is needed that provides a framework for inclusive and collaborative multi- and intercultural partnership.[13] This place should aim to further the growth of a migration-shaped mission that lays the foundations for a common understanding of the context and content of multicultural mission. It should address where and in what ways migrants have a voice in a migration-shaped church and in its mission; what their role should be in shaping a new ecclesial landscape that transcends traditional patterns of ecumenical cooperation of well-established local churches.

39. Ecclesial identities are important sources of faith and ministry. However, these identities should also be subject to transformation in the light of Christ who migrated from heaven to earth and who crossed human divides. In carrying out its migration-shaped mission, the church has no choice but to transcend its confessional, national and cultural boundaries. The church as a pilgrim community knows that failing to humbly transcend given boundaries and divides will result in a failure to shape a welcoming space for all sojourners.

40. As a divine migrant, the incarnate Christ crossed the boundary from eternity into the "broken territory of human life."[14] During his life on earth, he constantly crossed boundaries and called people to cross boundaries in order to have a foretaste of the reign of God and to overcome otherness. He called every human to partake in the celebration of love, affirmation of dignity and realization of justice. This is God's call to the church as well. Pilgrims – local residents and migrants alike – share responsibility to partake in this mission to shape inclusive communities that can transform human lives into God's restored image.

---

[13] See the report of the WCC consultation on the mission and ecclesiology of migrant/multicultural churches, Utrecht, November 2010, in: *IRM*, April 2011, 100.1 (392), 104-107.
[14] D.G. Groody, *Crossing the Divide*, 651.

3. ECUMENICAL RESPONSES

Koinonia, Leitourgia, Martyria *and* Diakonia:
Ecclesial Steps on the Journey toward Justice and Transformation

41. Being the church in different geographical, socio-political, cultural and economic settings requires a critical analysis of the situation the migrant church finds itself in so that ecclesial responses can be developed that are context- and justice-sensitive. The following suggestions for ecclesial responses are therefore of a rather general character, are inconclusive and incomplete in nature and more in the form of an invitation to develop specific regional responses. They are laid out utilizing the classical notion of the church unfolding its nature and mission in *koinonia, martyria, leitourgia* and *diakonia*.

Koinonia: The Church in Communion

42. Romans 12 and 1 Corinthians 12 picture the church as a tapestry of diversity – "we, who are many, are one body in Christ" (Romans 12:5), in relationship with God and in relationship with one another. The church as a diverse community is inclusive and welcoming in nature and mission. The *oikonomia*, the household of God, is all-embracing and draws us into a committed communion, transcending geographical and human-made barriers so that none of us is any longer "a stranger or an alien, but [we] are citizens with the saints and also members of the household of God, built upon the foundation of the apostles and prophets, with Christ Jesus himself as a cornerstone" (Ephesians 2:19f.).

43. We acknowledge and we confess that many of our church communities are far from being inclusive communities, reflecting the one diverse Body of Christ, as quite a number of our structures, practices and teachings are themselves excluding, marginalizing and "othering," and are thus tearing the very Body of Christ apart.

44. Witnessing to the hope that is within us (1 Peter 3:15), we strive toward justice and transformation within our church communities and within society and the world at large. Living out unity and diversity as an inclusive community calls for:

- congregations to strive toward the larger unity as the one Body of Christ;

- churches to become culturally, socially and ethnically inclusive communities, embracing people of diverse cultural, social, economic and ethnic backgrounds;

- parishes or congregations that are safe places and inclusive, justice-oriented communities;

- increased intercultural and interreligious dialogue;

- the realization of a deeper ecumenism that refrains from "othering" and seeks mutuality, justice and shalom;

- a commitment to a migration-, justice- and transformation-oriented ecumenism that can give shape to inclusive, participatory and equal communities.

Leitourgia: The Church in Service

45. A church as a celebrating community on the way, as sojourners on earth, seeks to serve God, humanity and creation, is called in for worship and sent out to perform the "liturgy after the liturgy."

46. We acknowledge and we confess that many of our church communities are far from being inclusive church in service and celebration with and for all of humanity and creation. Our *leitourgia* is often merely vertically oriented, leaving aside issues of justice and transformation as well as the experiences of suffering of so many, especially in the context of migration.

47. Witnessing to the hope that is within us (1 Peter 3:15), we strive toward justice and transformation within our church communities and within society and the world at large. Being an inclusive church in service calls for:

- a move beyond the mono-cultural paradigm that often characterizes worship services;

- an understanding of worship that exceeds a Sunday-celebration gathering;

- a liturgy that is aware of being the church on the way as well as sensitive to the experiences, sufferings, hopes and aspirations of people in situations of migration;

- texts, sermons, Bible studies and prayers that address migration-related issues of justice and transformation;

- days of prayer and action related to people in migrant situations, refugees and internally displaced people;

- special memorial services for the victims of national and transnational migration, e.g., recalling those who died during sea transfers and crossings.

Martyria: The Church in Witness

48. The church as a witnessing community is testifying to the challenging character of the inclusive kingdom of God. In word and deed, it announces the good news to the poor, liberty to the captives, recovery of sight to the blind and freedom to the oppressed (Luke 4:18-19).

49. We acknowledge and we confess that many of our church communities are far from practising *martyria* as a public witness that draws attention to issues of oppression, destruction, death and human rights violations in the context of migration or in other areas, such as the global economic (dis)order, that threaten the life and livelihood of the majority population on this globe.

50. Witnessing to the hope that is within us (1 Peter 3:15), we strive toward justice and transformation within our church communities and within society and the world at large. Witnessing to the challenging character of the kingdom of God calls for:

- being a migrant church at the margins and of the margins, based on Jesus' holistic mission that was placing those who had been marginalized for ethnic, cultural, health, economic or socio-political reasons at the centre-stage of his kingdom and mission;

- a stronger involvement in advocacy on migration issues;

- an affirmation of migrant agency;

- a public critique of structures and practices that further and contribute to the "othering," the discrimination and the violation of human beings, particularly of those on the move;

- a strengthening of pastoral as well as political responses with regard to migration, justice and human rights;

- intensive training in migrant and intercultural ministries as part of the theological education and formation of pastors.

Roma in Germany

The situation of individuals and families with Roma background is, in many countries, a very challenging and volatile one. For example, in the German context, the level of anti-Roma in the general population is extremely high, leading to unequal and disadvantaging treatment in basically all relevant aspects of life, ranging from social support services to education.

Migrants with a Roma background often live in conditions of extreme poverty, with job opportunities mostly limited to the 3D-sector. Payment received is poor, often not even covering the basic needs related to food security, basic housing and clothing. Amongst migrant groups, Roma families are particularly vulnerable to eviction and expulsion by landlords and landladies. Roma families are often seen as "beggars" and "criminal elements," and especially children and youth frequently face physical and verbal acts of violence in the streets.

To improve the living conditions as well as the integration of families of Roma background in Berlin's intercultural Neukoelln borough, the local Methodist congregation has embarked on a programme that offers:

- a safe place for children with migration background, accessible five days a week; language courses on the premises of the church as well as at the local primary school; language courses for parents, particularly mothers;

- homework supervision and support in coping with the school curricula; accompaniment and support for negotiations e.g., with social services, regional offices of home affairs, schools or landlords and landladies;

- general advocacy to foster awareness of the special situation migrant families and their children, particularly of a Roma background, find themselves in, and space for interreligious and intercultural encounter and support in the process of inclusion.

The activities of the congregation are based on the Methodist social creed. The congregation is part of larger networks of NGOs and faith-based organizations.

Diakonia: The Church in Action

51. The church as a diaconal community is characterized by transformative action. The model for our diaconal ministry is Jesus Christ who holistically and in challenging ways met the needs and the quests for inclusion, justice and life in its fullness of those he encountered. Feeding the hungry, quenching the thirst of the thirsty, receiving the "stranger," clothing the naked, taking care of the sick and visiting the prisoner (Matthew 25:35-40) are as much part and parcel of the diaconal work of the church as is the search for structures and practices in which justice prevails, human potential can be developed, and where human, individual and communitarian rights, mutuality and equality are essentially grounded.

52. We acknowledge and we confess that many of our church communities are far from a consistent involvement in transformative action that seeks justice wherever individual deeds and socio-economic structures and practices mar and harm the human being, particularly in the context of migration. We have fed the hungry, sheltered the homeless, dressed the wounds of the violated, but often failed to question the structures and practices causing violation and harm, in migration as well as in socio-economic issues at large. Our diaconal outreach was often based on a charitable rather than on a justice paradigm.

53. Witnessing to the hope that is within us (1 Peter 3:15), we strive toward justice and transformation within our church communities and within society and the world at large. Being a church in transformative action calls for:

- joining hands with civil, societal and faith-based organizations in addressing the root causes of migration – war, poverty and climate change;

- redressing structures and practices that disadvantage, exclude and endanger people's lives;

- together with people of all faiths, setting up structures of an international *diakonia* that is strongly geared toward issues of migration and justice;

- fostering local social action and support for migrants;

- expressing special solidarity with the migrants whose status is "unauthorized" by a nation-state.

54. *Koinonia, leitourgia, martyria* and *diakonia* are public expressions of the faith and the hope of the one, holy, catholic and apostolic church, the diverse and yet united body of Christ. The hope that is within us (1 Peter 3:15) drives us on our way toward becoming just and inclusive communities, the migrant church at large.

"Witnessing Together" Geneva

Churches stemming from migration have been in Geneva since the early days of the Reformation. Over the last decades, their number has grown, and today they hold a significant place in Geneva Protestantism. About ten years ago, Lukas Vischer initiated the intercultural movement "Witnessing together," hoping that diverse church communities would join hands and forge links with one another. After a number of meetings, the first joint service in Geneva took place in 2003 at St Peter's cathedral. Joint services have since united communities that share the same place of worship or that are active in the same area.

"Witnessing together" brings together about a hundred communities of every geographical origin and all trends of Protestantism, including some of the Orthodox churches, with the "historic" Protestant Church of Geneva (EPG), of which many members have links with the movement. The coordinator of this movement, Reverend Roswitha Golder, honourary pastor of the Protestant Church of Geneva who served the Latin-American community of Onex for twelve years, identifies three aims of this movement:

– Learn to know each other by visiting each other;

– Organize regular meetings and discussions for the mutual enrichment of the communities;

– Lead joint activities.

Currently more than half of the "historic" Protestant Churches in Geneva are sharing their buildings and facilities with one or more migrant communities.

---

55. Justice and transformation are at the heart of quite a number of prophetic writings and of the ministry of Jesus. Working and walking toward justice and transformation has been an ongoing challenge and a continuous journey for the church throughout the centuries and is a particular challenge for the church amidst migration today.

56. On a number of occasions in history, the church has halted and taken time to reflect upon its biblical points of departure, the routes and directions it has pursued and the cul-de-sacs it has ventured into, deviating from its original pursuit. The current realities of migration challenge the church to come to a halt once again and to reflect on what being a just, inclusive and transformative community implies within the community of believers as well as with regard to the world at large.

57. While some of our church communities have lived up to the challenge of being just, inclusive and transformative communities in word and deed, other church communities find themselves still at the very beginning of the road, indecisive at major intersections or lost in detours and thus manifesting the status quo of a dividing and marginalizing world. We give thanks for the courage of those church communities fearlessly leading the way toward justice and transformation, and we acknowledge and confess the shortcomings and failures of many others of our church communities.

58. We confess that

   - as church communities. we have often been complacent in exclusion and injustice through structures, practices, services and worship;

   - we have been slow to get started to make our church and municipal communities inclusive and participatory ones;

   - "othering" has been part of our theological heritage and rationale;

- our understanding of being the church was more impacted by ethnic and cultural issues than the notion of the migrant church at large or the migrant and refugee Jesus Christ;

- mission has often been understood in mere terms of spiritual conversion, with the wider holistic transformative aspects of *missio Dei* being largely ignored;

- issues of migration, justice, inclusivity and transformation have frequently been relegated to so-called "non-theological issues", therefore scarcely impacting our practices, teachings and outreach;

- we were often fearful in our advocacy, reluctant in justice-oriented action and failing to speak truth to power.

59. For these and for many other failures and shortcomings, we ask for God's forgiveness. We commit ourselves to the whole gospel pathway of justice, reconciliation and transformation, and we ask for God's guidance as, renewed and strengthened, we once again embark on the journey toward practicing justice and transformation. Witnessing to the hope that is within us (1 Peter 3:15), we strive toward justice and transformation within our church communities and within society and the world at large. We do so as followers of the migrant Christ who said: "I am the way, the truth and the life" (John 14:6) and who came "so that all may have life and have it in abundance" (John 10:10).

APPENDIX. MIGRATION TODAY

Migration: Constant and Changing

60. Responding to the impact of migration is urgent. To the privileged few, migration may be a "good experience," but to most migrants, the realities imply hardships: being uprooted, detained, trafficked or even dying on the journey. While migration has always been a feature of human existence, the migration phenomenon over the last 60 years is one of the most influential forces impacting the demographic, social, cultural, religious and economic landscapes of nations throughout the world. Today, the movement of people occurs in multiple directions across the globe. It is a complex phenomenon: each person on the move has their own story and journey filled with sorrow, hope and aspirations. The purpose of this paper is to call churches to realize the urgency and to act accordingly within their context by framing adequate responses.

The Story of the Mission for Migrant Workers and the Asia Pacific Mission for Migrants

In the late 1970s amidst the intensifying socio-economic, political and cultural crisis gripping the Philippines, the government started a vigorous deployment of its people abroad both for the financial returns from labour export as well as to stave off the potential social upheaval due to widespread poverty, unemployment and landlessness. The Labour Export Programme (LEP) was instituted by then-Pres. Ferdinand Marcos. It paved the way for more semi-skilled and unskilled workers to be deployed to countries in need of the cheap, flexible and docile labour that foreign workers can provide in their booming industries and in their service sector, particularly domestic work. Hong Kong was one of the areas where workers were rapidly deployed as it opened its doors to foreign domestic workers, mostly women.

This development did not escape the notice of church leaders. In coordination with the Resource Centre for Philippine Concerns (RCPC), a church-backed NGO in Hong Kong at that time, the National Council of Churches in the Philippines (NCCP) and the Anglican Holy Carpenter Church (HCC) arranged for a lay missionary to come to Hong Kong in 1980 to research the condition of migrant workers and explore the possibility of creating a service ministry organization. Based on the investigation and recommendations of the lay missionary, a series of consultations were conducted on how an ecumenical centre for migrants could be established. Finally in March 1981, a proposal drawn up by the NCCP as an endorsing institution in the Philippines and the HCC as a sponsor to establish a Mission for Filipino Migrant Workers (MFMW) was realized.

The MFMW immediately began its work of delivering assistance to migrants in crisis together with programmes that aim to empower migrant workers in Hong Kong. By 1983, in the face of the intensified LEP, the MFMW recommended that the NCCP study the possibility of replicating the MFMW experience in other Asia-Pacific countries. The NCCP took up the recommendation and set up the Asia-Pacific Mission for Migrant Filipinos (APMMF) to operate in countries in the region, including the Middle East. The APMMF started its work in 1984.

Later on, the MFMW and the APMMF were renamed Mission for Migrant Workers and the Asia Pacific Mission for Migrants, respectively, to denote the expansion of its work among migrants of different nationalities.

61. Nation-states are becoming increasingly diverse. National and regional immigration policies often tend to label and criminalize migrants as "problems" and populist media debates exacerbate such notions of superiority and inferiority. Simply labeling a person "migrant," "asylum-seeker" or "displaced" creates harmful categories

that this work seeks to overcome. Migrant groups are divided into those who are "wanted" and those who are not, and sophisticated and complex mechanisms of inclusion and exclusion have been developed. In other words, notions of "us" versus "them" and "we" versus "others" are frequently implied in migration-related debates and policy-making, which are not helpful in the conversation.

62. Governments of sending and receiving countries recognize the strategic importance, economic benefit, and complexities of global migration and have intensified their resolve to find appropriate political responses. These policies tend to protect the economic and social impact on the receiving country while relegating the migrant to the margins of society. The UN, while recognizing that migration continues to increase, provides a platform for strategic analysis and strategizing. It aims to promote respect for the human rights of migrants, and to contribute to peaceful integration of migrants in society. In doing so, it wants to "build a better migration experience" and to ensure that "people move in a way that is safe and legal, and which protects their rights."[1]

63. Churches are therefore not alone in their efforts to respond to the impact of migration. With many others who affirm life and who strive for justice and peace, churches are involved in many local, national and international activities. Churches are involved in lobbying and advocacy, they speak up for migrants held in detention, they participate in the debate on migration and they establish multicultural congregations for those who have migrated. Challenges involve both ethical and ecclesial issues, such as claiming justice for migrants and creating ample space for emerging migrant churches in local ecumenical structures. We believe that in order to act and respond in a just and life-affirming way to the challenges we face in our contexts, it is vital to start by affirming that human beings are created in the image and likeness of God (Gen 1:26). Every individual – whether on the move or settled – is deserving of life, love and dignity.

---

[1] UN General-Secretary Bang-Ki Moon, at the Global Forum on Migration and Development, July 10, 2007.

64. This paper has been divided into three sections. The first section explored biblical and theological perspectives, while the second section identified the subsequent implications for the nature and mission of the church. The core document concluded with a call for a renewed ecumenical response to migration in the light of the WCC 2013 Assembly theme, "God of life lead us to Justice and Peace." In this last section, we introduce the migration phenomenon and discuss its facets and ambivalences.

Who Is on the Move?

65. Migration is a global phenomenon involving an increasing array of ethnic and cultural groups. The term "migrant" comprises categories such as migrant workers and their families, professionals, international students, refugees, asylum-seekers, internally displaced persons and victims of human trafficking.

66. There are many reasons why people migrate. For some, the decision to migrate is made voluntarily, while horrific events often compel others to move. Some migrants may feel their motivation lies somewhere between these two points. For example, severe environmental factors such as drought create great uncertainty about remaining in their home countries. Others may feel that their decision is made voluntarily but may be strongly motivated to move rather than remain and endure intolerable conditions. The term "economic migrants" is often used to distinguish between forced and voluntary movement. In contrast to refugees, economic migrants can normally return home if they choose to, enjoying freedom from the threat of persecution, and can generally seek the protection of their national government. Others face disparities in living conditions between nations that impact their decision to migrate. These factors include a range of both positive and negative aspects concerning the decision to leave and the choice of destination. Often when migration flows have started, there is a tendency for the movement to continue.

67. Today, more than 215 million people live outside their countries of origin or citizenship. The majority of international migrants (about 90 percent) are migrant workers and their families.[2] Of the total number of international migrants, 72 percent are of working age (20 to 64) and around half (49 percent) are women[3]; 105 million men and women are economically active and a similar number are children and other dependents accompanying working migrants.[4] The majority (96 million) of working age international migrants reside in developed countries. For migrants seeking employment, strong demand encourages many (especially from labour-exporting countries such as Mexico, India, China and the Philippines) to migrate to places with a growing economy. This can be mutually beneficial as some countries require highly skilled workers and international students. Meanwhile, other countries seek migrant labour to meet the growing demand in their labour, manufacturing, construction, and service industries. International migrants comprise 3 percent of the global population, and this trend is expected to continue, meaning that migrant numbers will increase as the world population increases.

68. The United Nations stated that in 2008, 20 million people worldwide were forced to migrate due to extreme climate-related weather events, environmental deterioration, natural disasters, rising sea levels, and severe weather patterns such as drought.[5] Several reports predict that rising sea levels, desertification, soil erosion and shrinking freshwater supplies – all made worse by climate change – could displace up to 50 million people within the next ten years. Although these migrants may be forced permanently from their homelands, they do not meet the criteria for refugee status established by the 1951 UN Convention on Refugees and are not recognized under any other international agreement. For the indigenous people who share a special connection to their homeland, the impact of environmental degradation is devastating. When they are expelled from the land of their ancestors,

---

[2] *International Labour Migration: A Rights Based Approach.* International Labour Organization, 2010 Geneva, 4.

[3] *Population Facts* 6, 1UN Department of Economics and Social Affairs, Population Division 2010.

[4] *International Labour Migration: A Rights Based Approach.* International Labour Organization (ILO) 2010, Geneva, 4.

[5] *Monitoring disaster displacement in the context of climate change.* United Nations Office for the Coordination of Humanitarian Affairs (OCHA) 2009, Internal Displacement Monitoring Centre (IDMC), Geneva, 12.

they lose their sacred places and many are condemned to the margins of society, often living in slums, without the structures to improve their conditions.

69. Many people are compelled to migrate for mere survival or to obtain sufficient living conditions for survival elsewhere. They are forced to leave their homes due to state or group violence, war and conflict, political instability, poverty, human rights violations, gender violence, lack of freedom (including religious freedom) and rights of participation. According to the United Nations High Commissioner for Refugees (UNHCR), there are currently approximately 15 million refugees worldwide, and almost one million asylum-seekers are awaiting the outcome of their claim for refugee status. A refugee is someone, according to the 1951 UN Convention on Refugees, who "owing to a well-founded fear of being persecuted for reasons of race, religion, nationality, membership of a particular social group or political opinion, is outside the country of his nationality, and is unable to, or owing to such fear is unwilling to, avail himself of the protection of that country."[6]

70. In addition to the 215 million international migrants, a further 12 million people are stateless and another 26.4 million are displaced internally due to conflict.[7] Unlike refugees, IDPs have not crossed an international border to find sanctuary but have remained inside their home countries. Statelessness refers to the condition of an individual who is not considered as a national by any state. Stateless people face numerous difficulties in their daily lives: they can lack access to health care, education, property rights and the ability to move freely.

---

[6] Article 1A (2) of the *Convention Relating to the Status of Refugees* (1951).
[7] *Global Trends 2011*. United Nations High Commissioner for Refugees (UNHCR), Geneva, 2-5.

A Displaced Family in Haiti

Marie Nicole is 34, a mother of three children. Until recently she, together with her three children, lived in a tent made of scraps of bed sheets. "After the earthquake, I thought life was over and I would never own a decent place to live with my children," Marie Nicole said. "I had no choice and settled in my little tent of sheets supported by wood sticks. We had to squeeze like fish at the market to sleep at night."

Living in the tent was tough. It was extremely hot during the day and cold at night. When the rains and the wind came, Marie Nicole and her children were forced to stay awake at night to hold up the supports of their flimsy shelter. They suffered through many sleepless nights.

Marie Nicole's new upgradable shelter was constructed by Habitat for Humanity with support from United Methodist Committee on Relief (UMCOR) and partners. "Now I'm not worried about the wind and rains. I can sleep with both eyes closed and my children will grow in a better environment, cleaner and safer," Marie Nicole said.

She now earns a living as a merchant and holds her head up high with dignity.

71. As the following graph indicates, migrants are often categorized. Categories cannot capture all the complexities of a constantly evolving phenomenon and the unique nature of each migrant experience, yet we nevertheless make use of them. While we cannot reduce suffering experienced by migrants to categories, figure 1 below nevertheless helps us to deduce the impact of migration.

Fig 1: 2010 Global Total Number of Migrants by Category

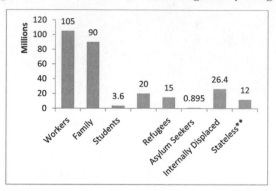

Data Source: ILO International Labour Migration: A Rights-Based Approach 2010, UNHCR Global Trends 2011. *UNOCHA 2009 Estimate for 2008. **Stateless people are not necessarily migrants.

72. The migration phenomenon has increased exponentially in the last 60 years, not only due to technological advances supporting transport and communication, but primarily because it has been vastly fueled by a shift in economic hegemony. The West, which was once the world's workshop, has now become the world's consumer while the East has become the world's workshop. Most migrants reach their destination in full accordance with the laws and regulations of the origin and destination countries and make their journey safely and easily. The journeys of other migrants will be much more perilous. Often people on the move will switch categories from regular to irregular status and vice versa as they juggle the demands of international movement and the necessities of life. Below we mention three more types of migration.

73. Irregular migration takes place outside the norms and procedures established by nation-states to manage the orderly flow of migrants into, through and out of their territories. Those who gain access into a country of their choice often begin their new life indebted and face a life of inhospitality, uncertainty and inhumane conditions. The vast majority of migrants with irregular status often get detained on arrival and deported after a short asylum procedure.

74. Trafficking in human beings is active and wilful "recruitment, transportation, transfer, harbouring or receipt of persons, by means of the threat or use of force or other forms of coercion, of abduction, of fraud, of deception, of the abuse of power or of a position of vulnerability or of the giving of payments or benefits to achieve the consent of a person having control over another person for the purpose of exploitation."[8] The majority of trafficked migrants are exposed to violence and abuse along their journey. Victims of trafficking are prone to exploitation, particularly sexual and labour exploitation. Female migrants and migrant children are particularly vulnerable.

75. People-smuggling is a form of cross-border movement that is facilitated with the agreement of the migrant who usually pays for the smuggling services. Smuggling can be exploitative and dangerous, and sometimes fatal, but it has been chosen rather than coerced. The Palermo Protocols which govern international law on people-smuggling define these services as felonious when organized criminal groups are taking a leading role.

Migration and Economic Emancipation

76. Poverty has become a leading factor in the decision to migrate and also allows for the sending of remittances which can raise living standards of family members left at home. Some governments such as those of the Philippines and India actively promote labour migration; these countries benefit from huge economic benefits through remittances which have become an important part of the national income. On the other hand, migration separates many families, leading to the breakdown of family structures. In addition, many sending countries experience what is termed as "brain drain," with some of their brightest and best citizens opting to leave and never returning.

77. However, this paper does not contend that migration itself is the problem but rather the inequality of wealth and power under which migration practices unfold. This has led to exploitation and

---

8 Protocol to Prevent, Suppress and Punish Trafficking in Persons, Especially Women and Children, supplementing the United Nations Convention against Transnational Organized Crime.

marginalization of many groups.[9] The underlying issue for the church is the ability of all humans to live in dignity; an unattained goal in the face of extreme poverty. In all probability, greater equality achieved through development will make the option to migrate more available as a voluntary instead of a forced or compelled choice.

78. The growth of capitalism and globalization has raised the living standards of many people while at the same time increasing inequality and the number of working poor. Greater equality can be achieved through concerted migration policies which do not exclude the poor and low-skilled workers. As new labour markets open up, the participation of the poor can lead to higher incomes and higher remittances sent back to poorer sending countries. In 2010, the World Bank estimated the value of remittances to be around $US440 billion dollars, of which $US325 billions went directly to developing nations.[10] However, for more liberal labour markets which include the poor to actually translate into greater equality, it is essential that the worker rights of immigrants be guaranteed, and protected by destination countries. Dangerous working conditions, lax safety and health protection continue to result in death and injury of migrants. Too often, companies choosing to manufacture their products in lax environments have increased the profitability for shareholders while driving down salaries and creating hardships for migrant workers.

Family Concerns

79. The migration regime poses multiple challenges to the family as the core cultural, social and economic unit in society. Families prepare the next generations for the world of work, but they experience that migration impacts the spiritual condition of all involved in a harmful way. Many migrant workers have to leave husbands or wives and children behind in order to work abroad to provide for them. In some cases, both parents must go abroad to work and have no choice but to leave the care of their children in the hands of others. Many families start their respective journeys by selling belongings and property or by taking out loans, leading them into considerable debt.

---

[9] S. Castles, *Understanding Global Migration: A Social Transformation Perspective*. Conference on Theories of Migration and Social Change, St Anne's College, Woodstock Road, Oxford, July 1-3, 2008.

[10] *World Bank's Migration and Remittances Factbook 2011*, http://go.worldbank.org/QGUCPJTOR0.

Intergenerational tension between older and younger family members can occur. In the process of adapting to the new cultural context, they have to mark new identity boundaries, while having to cope with issues like the use of the native or a new language, different views of religion, authority structures, education, gender issues and the like.

Tension and Exclusion

80. When migrants begin to settle in a new environment, emerging identity differences – national, religious, ethnic or cultural – can become serious causes of tensions between migrants and receiving communities. Migrant communities often express their own practices, languages, dress and moral codes in a desire to hold on to what is important to them from home. Sometimes, in response, receiving communities resist or mistreat outsiders for the fear that the other's identity poses a threat to their own identities or culture. Above all, religious and national identities have been the source of tensions and xenophobia in many contexts. Some right-wing groups, aspiring to intimidate and control migrant communities, employ xenophobic arguments to create an environment of hatred, suspicion and division between communities.

Exploitation

81. Migrants can be vulnerable to exploitation in receiving countries whenever they are perceived as "other" or of lesser value, and where such attitudes have been structurally embedded through lack of labour/employment and other laws to protect those with or without authorization to be there. In their search for better living conditions, migrants are often treated and traded as commodities, for example in individual homes as domestic workers or in factories. Trafficking for labour or sexual exploitation and for human organ removal is perhaps the most extreme violation of the dignity of the person and sanctity of life given by God.

> ### Racism
>
> Racism can range from cultural superiority/inferiority debates to hate speech, physical attacks and sociocides or genocides. Structural racism bars equal access to work, education and services and hinders equal participation, involvement in decision-making and freedom of expression in pluralistic societies.
>
> "Othering" of migrants happens when we emphasize differences negatively over and above valuing commonalities or mutuality positively. "Othering" or stereotyping is a process in which mental, psychological and physical fences are constructed to keep out what and whoever appears to be "strange." The "other" is seen as a "non-fit," as "strange(r)" and as not meeting the requirements or nature of the "in-group." In a search for clear-cut identities, "othering" excludes, inferiorizes and very often hurts and violates those who are not admitted to the "in-group" and into the dominant players' culture(s) and discourses. As such, "othering" can pave the way toward racist attitudes and practices.

In July 2010, the GEM Regional Meeting in Bangkok reported:

Having heard stories of blatant exploitation and abuse of migrant workers in many of our regions and countries and also by making ourselves aware of such situations around the world, we reflected on the human tendency to exploit the vulnerability of the weak and the disempowered that goes on at various levels. Governments, structures, systems, communities, families and persons are tainted by this tendency which unfortunately stands out as the most shameful trait of our human civilization. Abuse, rape, trafficking and new forms of slavery, etc., all have their roots in this trait, and we as churches must recognize that we are a part of this sinful ethos and must seek forgiveness from God for our complicity and begin to rectify it by standing in solidarity with those who are thus denied of the opportunity of life with dignity and basic necessities.